ISBN 978-1-331-49862-9
PIBN 10198300

This book is a reproduction of an important historical work. Forgotten Books uses
state-of-the-art technology to digitally reconstruct the work, preserving the original format
whilst repairing imperfections present in the aged copy. In rare cases, an imperfection in
the original, such as a blemish or missing page, may be replicated in our edition. We do,
however, repair the vast majority of imperfections successfully; any imperfections that
remain are intentionally left to preserve the state of such historical works.

1 MONTH OF
FREE
READING

at

www.ForgottenBooks.com

By purchasing this book you are eligible for one month membership to ForgottenBooks.com, giving you unlimited access to our entire collection of over 700,000 titles via our web site and mobile apps.

To claim your free month visit: www.forgottenbooks.com/free198300

English
Français
Deutsche
Italiano
Español
Português

www.forgottenbooks.com

Mythology Photography **Fiction**
Fishing Christianity **Art** Cooking
Essays Buddhism Freemasonry
Medicine **Biology** Music **Ancient
Egypt** Evolution Carpentry Physics
Dance Geology **Mathematics** Fitness
Shakespeare **Folklore** Yoga Marketing
Confidence Immortality Biographies
Poetry **Psychology** Witchcraft
Electronics Chemistry History **Law**
Accounting **Philosophy** Anthropology
Alchemy Drama Quantum Mechanics
Atheism Sexual Health **Ancient History**
Entrepreneurship Languages Sport
Paleontology Needlework Islam
Metaphysics Investment Archaeology
Parenting Statistics Criminology
Motivational

PREFACE

If so it haps this little book shall be
A comfort to some friend I may not see,
Or if sometime, in God's Eternity,
Someone shall say: "I read your book one day,
When clouds so thick o'er-shadowed all my way,
There could not struggle through a single ray,
And suddenly there came a comfort sweet
Into my heart, and straight, on wingèd feet,
I sought some other bruisèd heart to meet,
That I might halve my morsel of content,
Before its life was utterly forespent,
When, lo, it seemed to grow, where're I went,
And then I said: 'God sent that book to me,
That I to someone else might comfort be,' "
I think I shall be glad eternally!

CONTENTS

A SONG OF THE DEEP

AND OTHER VERSES

AVE ATQUE VALE

HAIL and farewell! Is this your dismal creed?
Is life a vapor, flying swift away,
And yielding promise of no longer day?
Nor love and friendship still its greatest need?
And know we not what way our paths may lead?
Are we but ships that pass within a night
That yields no token of a coming light?
Nor is to-day to-morrow's root and seed?
Nay, but for me, farewell and then—all hail!
Because I live ye too shall live, said One,
And when I am there ye shall also be.
Those gone before—I follow in their trail,
And there shall be no more a setting sun,
But rich content as I their faces see.

THE PALMS OF ELIM

THE palms of Elim, lifting lucious dates
Aloft in air, and waving emerald wands
In bold defiance, though the desert mates
With stalking, cruel death their living fronds!
How have you triumphed o'er the ages fled
Since Moses to your shade God's people led!

Full weary were they of the shifting sands,
Whose blistering heat burned eyes, and throat
    and feet,
And oft they longed for Egypt's green-robed
    lands,
Where lavish bounty yielded meat to eat,
But when the palms of Elim welcome waved,
They shouted, in high chorus: "We are saved!"

And dost thou journey through a desert drear,
Whose treacherous sands yield but a scorching
    heat?
And dost thou miss old scenes, and faces dear,
That once were ever near thine eyes to greet?
Look up, faint heart, the palms of Elim still
Yield healing balm for every earthly ill!

THE WELCOME

THE welcome songs of heaven! How sweet they
    sound
To those new-born upon the mystic shore!
Not chanted sure by angels who surround
The throne of God; nay, those gone on before,
They only are assigned to this glad part,
Since they know best the native human heart.

Nor yet are they who long have known heaven's
    ways
Permitted first our loved and lost to greet.
Their voices now are tuned to God's high praise,
And so they have forgotten how to meet
Those who are strangers quite to lofty themes,
That they have grown familiar with, it seems.

Quite sure am I that children, come of late,
Are those who welcome children to that strand.
They have not yet forgotten how to mate
Their song to thoughts that children under-
    stand.
Alas, that you and I forget so soon
The ways we trod when shod by little shoon!

And mothers lately come to heaven, I think,
Are those who welcome mothers to that bliss,
For they know best the songs that best can link
Our mothers, we no longer here may kiss,

To all the sweet, new rapture they shall know
In finding children lost to them below!

And fathers not yet grown familiar quite
With songs the Seraphim alone can teach,
They welcome fathers who have fought the fight,
But yet are strangers to the heavenly speech,
For they still understand the father heart,
And best can shape their song to such glad art.

I sometimes greatly wonder who will cry
At first a welcome to the heavenly shore,
To one who falters thitherward, as I,
Or undertake to teach me its high lore?
I hope someone not yet beyond the reach
Of shaping music to an infant's speech!

  .   .   .   .   .   .

What fancy, all unwelcome, this, I pray,
That strangers new-born to the bliss above,
Are first to welcome to eternal day
Souls just arrived?   Nay, send me those I love,
However long they've gazed upon God's face,
However long I've missed them from their place!

My father left me when I was a child.
Rare, rich and ripe his knowledge now, I ween;
Yet am I sure that he in accents mild
Will greet me first, no other in between!
Sometimes I seem to catch his voice e'en now,
And see the aureole glow upon his brow.

Then all too soon I saw a brother fall
In dread eclipse that I refuse to name.
He sure will never wait for me to call,
However great his wisdom now and fame.
Love has a language of its own, you see,
So he will be the second to welcome me.

And many other friends almost as dear
Have grown familiar with high praises there.
Still I am never troubled with a fear
That they have ceased to love and for me care.
The first to greet me on the golden strand
Will be who gave me here the warmest hand.

SLEEPING

"Not dead but sleeping," of a little child,
Said Jesus to her parents, frantic, wild
With grief, the maid so loving was and mild.

"Not dead but sleeping," let these words be
    sown
Wherever mothers weep a child just flown,
And fathers tighten lips that else would moan.

"Not dead but sleeping," surely it were meet
To chant such song in tones both strong and
    sweet
When caskets, heavy, are borne through the
    street.

"Not dead but sleeping," mark so every mound,
Where grass grows green, since Grief walks
    slowly round
And waters with her tears the heaving ground.

"Not dead but sleeping," they shall rise at last,
Awakened by the joyful trumpet blast,
For Death could not the Lord of Life hold fast.

"Not dead but sleeping," heaven knows no such
    phrase;
No night, no sleep, no parting of the ways,
But glad reunion, and unceasing praise.

LAZARUS

"HE sleepeth, our friend sleepeth," Jesus said,
"I go to wake him, whom men say is dead,
Though Death into captivity is led."

"And if he sleep he shall do well," replied
Disciples, slow to learn, with all beside,
How fluent human speech, with Christ to guide.

"Moreover, Jews of late to kill Thee sought,
And will Thou venture thitherward for naught,
And so endanger all Thy life hath wrought?"

Then said He plainly: "Lazarus is dead,
And I am glad his spirit thus is fled,
That you to stronger faith may now be led.

"Up, let us go and see where he is laid.
Since time began twelve hours a day have made.
Who follows Duty need not be afraid."

Then Thomas, at whom all men point in scorn,
As least in faith of all of woman born,
Showed courage radiant as the glowing morn;

Since this bold challenge to the rest he threw:
"The Master goes to meet his death, will you
Forsake Him, now that danger heaves in view?

"Nay, let us go and die, if need so be,
With Him who came from sin to set us free;
To whom we pledged age-long fidelity."

And so they started on this journey long,
Across the Jordan, up the steep where throng
Fierce robber chieftains, daily rue and wrong;

Till at the last to Bethany they came,
And Martha met Him with reproof and blame:
"If thou hadst been here all had been the same!"

Then Jesus said: "Thy brother shall arise."
"Yea," Martha answered, "at the last surprise
Of resurrection, I may well surmise!"

"I am the Resurrection," then said He,
"Believe in God, his glory thou shalt see,
Not in some shadowy future; now, by Me!"

Then hastened Martha, full of hope new-born,
To find her sister, sitting mute, forlorn,
Immured in night, and heedless of the morn.

"The Master comes and calls for thee," she
    said,
And to His feet her weeping sister led;
"Too late!" she cried, "my brother now is dead!"

Then Jesus wept, not tears of vain regret
That Lazarus the common fate had met;
His eyes with Sorrow's sympathy were wet.

Perhaps he sorrowed also thus to find
So little faith and trust, in human-kind,
So much of selfish grief, sin-led and blind.

But soon they came where Lazarus was laid,
And Jesus lifted up his eyes and prayed,
Then cried—"Come forth!" and Lazarus ar-
    rayed

In cerements came forth. "Loose him now," He
    cried,
"And set him free!" So God was glorified,
Joy lived anew, and grace was magnified.

It is a story old, yet ever new,
Preserved for us by one who saith it's true,
Who lived so near the Master's heart, he knew.

Why should we doubt that He, the Prince of
    Life,
Could thus bring back to scenes of mortal strife,
Those who had passed to where all joys are rife?

Why should we long, as longed those sisters
    fond,
For the return of those passed safe beyond,
And gained their freedom from earth's fretting
    bond?

[9]

"If ye but loved me," said One long ago,
"Ye would rejoice I to the Father go,
Since He is greater than all else, you know."

If we but loved our loved ones, as we think,
We should rejoice to have them break the link
That bound them to the pain from which we
  shrink.

Oh, vain self-love, that takes the holy name
Of love for others, and is ever fain
To keep them here, despite of toil and pain!

I dare to think the happiest lot on earth
Is no fair match for joy that comes to birth
What time God shows his satisfying worth!

I dare to say a triumph song should wing
Those we have loved to greet the Savior King;
Instead, blue rosemary and rue we bring!

GOD OF THE LIVING

Not of the dead, but of the living, Thou
Oh, God, art God! Alive forever more,
And basking in Thy presence even now
Are they whose going left our hearts so sore!

When men shall say of me: He now is dead,
Who was so much alive but yester-eve,
I shall in Christ's triumphal train be led,
Far more alive than I can now believe.

Dead to all sin, and sorrow, born of sin,
Dead to all loss through friends that faithless
    are,
But to all joy the pearly gates within,
Alive, and never more to suffer mar!

Thou, Prince of Life art mine and I am Thine;
Great price Thou gavest as my ransom fee.
Thou lovest not as man a little time;
If Thine to-day, Thine in eternity!

Why should I fear Thine Angel men call Death,
And shrink, as pagans do, from his embrace?
He takes my hand, and lo! within a breath,
I clasp Thy hand, I see Thy beauteous face!

THE SYRIAN PHYSICIAN

GREAT was the tumult in the Roman's home,
His wife distraught, his slaves with terror dumb,
Nor any sound of music, but the moan
Reiterant and constant of his son.

For many days upon his fevered cot
Moaning he'd lain and wasting towards the
    grave,
The skill of learned leeches virtued not
His fever to abate, his life to save.

At last a Hebrew servant, Abgar named,
Approached with fear the stern centurion:
"Master," said he, "thy leeches are far-famed,
And yet 'tis plain they cannot save thy son.

"I beg thee send for Christ of Gallilee,
The Nazarene physician of my race,
His magic cures on every hand I see,
His miracles in every lane I trace."

The Captain of the hundred bowed the head,
Broken was he with grief and worn with woe,
And willing now and ready to be led
To any rescue, or by friend or foe.

"Abgar," he said, "though slave thou art and
  Jew,
Thou speakest wisely and the truth I see,
Too long have fought against the truth I knew.
Thy Christ can heal my son and only He.

"Go thou at once and bring my swiftest steed,
And summon soldiers on to follow fast,
I ride o'er plain and mountain with all speed,
The Nazarene has conquered at the last."

For hours he flew through hamlet, city, town,
And up and down the hills of Galilee;
And now upon the pavement threw him down,
Where stood the Man of Simple Majesty.

"Master," he said, "my son e'en now is dead,
But Thou, they say, canst make the dead to
  live;
Need'st not to journey to his silent bed,
Speak Thou the word, and surely he shall live."

The Master smiling to the people spake:
"Such faith I've found, no not in Israel;"
And to the father: "What thou asketh take,
Rejoice, for sure thy son is sleeping well."

Quick mounted he again his foaming mare,
O'er plain and mountain rode for many a rood,
But e're he reached his lake-side city fair,
His servant met him and made glad his mood.

"Lo, thy son liveth," shouted he with glee!
"And when, I ask, did he begin to mend?"
" 'Twas yesterday the fever left," said he,
"At the ninth hour," and low his head did
     bend.

"The very hour He spake the word of grace,
The Nazarene, to whom thou badst me go!
Now know I that with your despisèd race,
There is a God who healeth every woe."
     .   .   .   .

It is a tale from out the storied past,
And strange it soundeth to our ears to-day;
This Christ they say was crucified at last,
And under Syrian skies for aye doth lay.

And yet to me He seemeth still to live,
His works of grace on every hand I trace,
We touch His seamless robe and lo! He gives
His healing virtue forth in every place.

And brows to-day sin's fever long has burned,
Are coolèd by His hands as formerly,
And men of will who long His will have
     spurned,
Are conquered by this man of Galilee.

And bodies that sin's leprosy hath marred
Are soothed to soundness by His tender palm,
And faces that the wine-cup long hath scarred
Transfigured are by his forgiving balm.

I too was blind, and lo, to-day I see,
For He mine eyes anointed of His grace.
I too a captive was, and now am free,
For He has lifted on me His fair face.

. . . .

And so you see I cannot think Him dead
And buried still beneath the Syrian stars.
'Tis written that He rose again and led
Captivity a captive from Death's bars!

Taste for thyself and see that He is good,
His hand is shortened not; He still can save;
His feast is spread, He welcomes all who would,
He lives for you, for whom His life He gave!

IN MEMORIAM OF ——

WE saw her bravely enter the dark valley;
  She knew release must be,
And yet a smile transfigured all her features,
  With beauty yet to be.

And evermore as deeper grew the shadow,
  Her face became more bright,
Until at last, at eventide, and darkness,
  She blossomed into light.

She had so much in this our world to live for,
  Life seemed so fair a fight,
She would have still continued in the battle,
  Yet said: "It is all right."

She was an artist soul, so found keen pleasure
  In every sound and sight;
In voice of music, bird, and brook and children,
  And silence of the night.

Her morn of life had not yet waxed to evening,
  Nor touched the highest noon;
Her task it seemed was left in incompleteness,
  And death came all too soon.

And yet when she was sure the master beckoned,
  She did not say Him—"nay,"
But went where hope is turned to full fruition,
  In an eternal day.

[16]

We drop our tears, we cannot cease from weep-
    ing;
So much has gone from life;
And yet for us the world will be the sweeter,
    With less of noise and strife.

For tears are not alone of grief and sorrow,
    The token of God's wrath;
They fall, as now, when some great, solemn joy,
    Is swept athwart our path.

For surely, only those we hold forever,
    In bonds that cannot break,
To whom we said, at the last, tender parting:
    "I'll meet you at the gate!"

Nor do they lose for us their proper being,
    Vaguely diffused through space;
Nor are they but a spark, now reunited
    To That which gave them grace.

Nor circle they in a far distant orbit,
    Or world that's yet to be;
Nor does their heaven lie neighborly about us,
    Only in infancy.

They walk with us, as ever, but more constant,
    Their voices, low and sweet,
Still speak to us, in all that is most sacred,
    And holy, as is meet.

The cloud of witnesses she now hath joined
   That still besets us round,
And so must we forever be courageous,
   Nor lacking faith be found.

And we must be, as was she, ever cheerful,
   Nor make of grief a bride,
For surely that would sorrow breed in heaven,
   Where now she doth abide.

They love her best who strive to be most like
      her,
   In all that's pure and fair;
Who run the race, as she did, but to conquer,
   Nor fight as beating air.

Her earthly race, as God had planned, is fin-
      ished:
   Bring laurel and bring bay,
For a fair brow, where pain had set his signet,
   And witness all, and say:

"We found it easy to believe in goodness,
   When in her company;
And we will try to lead the life heroic
   To grace her memory."

EVOLUTION

SAID Love to Life, "Take thou my hand,
And we will journey through the land,
O'er desert drear, up mountain steep,
Where you may often fall and weep,
Yet shall you never suffer wrong,
And we will wake each day with song,
 Just you and me, just you and me."

Said Life to Love, "With you beside,
I will not fear what may betide,
However hot or chill the day,
However long the weary way,
In sweet content still on we climb,
Up to the seraphim sublime,
From lowest animalcula,
 Just you and me, just you and me."

Said Love to Life, "The way we go
Is strewn with many a pang and throe,
Yet shall you never suffer pain
That reaps you not a priceless gain,
Since every pang and throe shall yield
The vantage of some higher field,
So go we on eternally
 Just you and me, just you and me."

Said Life to Love, "In you I know
The mother, father too, I trow
Of all that animates the seas,
And dwells in the immensities;

[19]

Of every bird, and beast and thing
That creeps, or flies on tiny wing,
Or nobler man that's yet to be,
    Through you and me, just you and me."

Said Love to Life, "The spiral winds,
Through lower forms and lesser minds,
And men and angels, up to God,
To highest bliss from lowest clod;
And I preside, o'er every birth
And death, that yields to higher worth;
So on we fare right merrily,
    Just you and me, just you and me."

Said Life to Love, "In thee I find
A recompense quite to my mind,
Of all that's bitter, such rare bliss
Is granted me through every kiss;
A joy is born of every woe,
And higher bliss from every throe
That sets the fettered prisoner free,
    Through you and me, just you and me."

Thus Life and Love, when time began,
Or ever they had fashioned man,
Set forth upon their journey, free
Of any fear that there could be
An end to that which God hath bound
In an eternal wedlock-round,
Or Life and Love could cease to be!
    Why should we fear, or you or me?

THE REVEALER

How true a portrait painter, he whose name
We speak in awe and fear, and hush our breath,
And call Revealer, as we try to frame
Some word that means the same, but is not
 Death!
A name well chosen since this artist's touch
Brings hidden worth to view upon the face,
Though cold and pallid, so we marvel much
That we had not before observed such grace.

A man I knew who earned the praise of men,
Through faithful toil in courts and civic place;
A studious man, and best belovèd when
Best known, who, as at length death touched
 his face,
Was so transfigured that we all exclaimed:
"Lo, one of Plutarch's heroes come again."

A JOURNEY

I JOURNEYED with a dear one, in the gloaming,
  Down in a valley deep;
For she was going where there is no moaning,
  Nor know they how to weep.

The way grew narrow, and we pressed the
      nearer,
  As onward still we went;
And she heard voices, ever growing clearer,
  That made her well content.

And there were hands, she thought of friends,
      who beckoned,
  From a far mountain peak;
And a vast portal glimmered for a second,
  But she was very weak!

And One unseen was walking close beside her,
  Who slipped our hands apart,
And ere I knew it I was groping for her,
  It was so very dark!

But nothing now can evermore bereave me;
  She is of me a part:
I see her not, yet she is ever with me;
  We lived so heart to heart.

And, as for me the day draws to its gloaming,
 The veil still thinner grows,
And I shall soon reach through the weak with-
   holding
 And clasp her hand; who knows?

THE EASTER EVANGEL

"He is not here," fond sister pure,
The tomb holds not his soul in thrall,
Immortal life is now made sure,
O listen to the Easter call!

"He is not here," O sorrowing one,—
The child whom illy you love well;
The grave imprisons not your son,
For glad has wrung the Easter bell.

"He is not here," O widowed heart,
Why do you do yourself such wrong?
Go, rather, toil within the mart,
For, lo, they chant the Easter song.

Let not the living seek the dead
Where outworn caskets merge in clay.
"Has risen!" Has risen!"—the living
    Head!
Shout! Shout for joy! An Easter day!

AT EVENTIDE

DARK all thy day? At eventide a star!
Our star at last shall glimmer from afar
To cheer thy way through all the dismal night,
Lest thou should'st fail in pressing towards the
    height.

One star of hope! At eventide! No more,
Since still by faith thou walkest, faint and sore;
More precious is faith's trial than pure gold,
Such is God's way of testing from of old.

"A sword," the angel said, "shall pierce thine
    heart,"
To Mary, set from womankind apart,
As Mother of the Christ-Child! And shalt thou
Escape, yet wear a crown upon thy brow?

Oh, trembling soul, no fate surpassing strange
Is thine; no path beyond the gracious range
Of God's pure purpose art thou called to tread.
Look up! The star of hope above thine head!

AT LAST

EACH man would have men say when they shall
    see
His face so pale, and murmur: "He is dead!"
"Here lies a man who never seemed to be
What he was not, nor was he fancy led
To think pretense a substitute for worth,
Nor barren life atoned by noble birth."

All men would fain be judged by what is best
Within them, since 'tis truest, so they think,
To what they are, though seeming lower quest
Has yielded them false gains they may not
    blink.
"Not what I seemed to be to hostile eye,
But what I dreamed of being!"—is their cry.

Young men see visions and old men dream
    dreams;
Moon-struck, we call them, visionary, wild!
Yet at the last it is our dreams it seems,
That hew us into shape, or brave or mild.
All men have longings to be fit and fine;
The final feast sets forth the best of wine.

THE COMMON LOT

GRANT me to share the common, human lot.
I ask not, Lord, that Thou remit a jot
Of pain, and granting joy, forget me not!

Have I not known the sweetest human bliss,
That angels envy, just a loving kiss?
Why should I ask then not to hear the hiss

Of serpents walking round in human guise,
The stab of envy, and the sad surprise
Of reputation blackened by surmise?

Of One we read: In Him we ever see
The dew of Youth, and: Perfected was He
By suffering consummated on the tree!

A lesser one, his servant, boasts his joy,
And tribulation too in high employ,
Made great by gladness and by deep annoy.

In sorrow, yet rejoicing evermore;
As poor, but riches adding to the score—
Repeated contradiction, o'er and o'er!

Blind Homer, and blind Milton greatly please.
Only the eye God-blinded ever sees;
And eloquence is born with mute Demonsthenes.

Nay, no one can nobility attain
Who knoweth not the sum of human pain,
And regal gladness both of heart and brain.

No picture beautiful can artist paint
Save light and shadow meet in sweet constraint;
Life is a web of deep content and plaint.

How shall I meet and talk with those I know
In the eternities, if I forego
The joy, the woe, that made their faces glow?

Or how companion in dim distant years
With those who serve and reign in other
        spheres,
Made great through mighty laughter and hot
        tears?

Nay let me fare with those who loyally
Have lived the life complex—a symphony
Of highest joy and deepest agony!

HIS SERVANTS SHALL SERVE HIM

WHAT is it that will constitute your heaven?
The crown? The "Well-done" by the Master
    spoken?
The purity no yeast of sin can leaven?
The white stone, and the new name given in
    token?

Perchance in harp and song will be your bliss,
For who could tire of praise to Him, our Friend,
Who suffered for us e'en the Judas kiss,
Whose tender flesh the cruel spear did rend?

It may be you of work are weary grown,
And long for rest that nevermore shall cease;
Too tired for casting crowns before the throne,
Your heaven will be just quietude and peace.

I find so much of joy in service here,
So great reward in toil of heart and hand,
Were there no work for me in heaven, I fear
I should not care to live in that fair land.

PARADOXES

WHEN I am weak, then am I strong,
  And cased in armor, in His name,
I conquer hoary-headed wrong,
  Though crowned with Infamy called Fame.

When I my will have yielded up,
  Then am I clothed with power divine;
And when I drink His bitter cup,
  I find it filled with sweetest wine.

When I am poor, then am I rich
  With wealth that Midas never knew;
And every night my tent I pitch
  On heights attained by but a few.

In persecution I find joy;
  I wear for crown the world's defame;
The darts of hell cannot annoy;
  He walketh with me through the flame.

When I am hungry I am fed
  With manna Moses never knew;
And in the wilderness am led
  By cloud and fiery pillar, too.

The valley of the shadow yields
  The comfort of Thy staff and rod;
A light to the celestial fields,
  A road triumphant to my God.

A SONG OF THE DEEP

THIS song came to me from the deep:
'Tis those I've loved and lost I keep;
The witching wand of memory
Forever brings them back to me;
'Tis those I've loved and lost I weep;
'Tis those I've lost I still do keep!

And they are with me on the land,
I reach and touch the vanished hand,
And they are with me on the deep,
Or if I wake, or if I sleep;
'Tis those I've loved and lost I weep;
'Tis those I've lost I still do keep!

SHOOTING STARS

Out of the void, into the night,
         You fly;
A flash, then into the void again.
         Oh, why?
Out of the void, into the night,
         A sigh;
Then out of the night into infinite light!
         So I!

WHERE WAS GOD?

THE eastern sky was all a glory then,
  What time, with knapsack filled and rifle
    swung
Upon the mountain, bare of creek or fen,
  On joy intent, forth from my home I flung
For a free day; on wingèd feet I trod;
    But where was God?

So young was I, with most of life to be,
  So much to learn, to see, to feel, to hear,
The lid of knowledge barely raised to see
  How rich her treasures are, and rare and
    dear;
And Death, unknown, forth stalking where I
    trod;
    But where was God?

A shot I did not hear, and instant night!
  The end of life, with life but just begun!
All hope cut off, and joy and blessed light,
  And everything for which life's race is run!
Gone all the world whereon my feet had trod!
    Where, where was God?

God was and is in all the glory dawn,
  And on the mountains high upreared of yore;
Joy in the bird, fear in the timorous fawn,

Death in the fatal shot! Since evermore
God walks all worlds where life and death have
trod;
There, there is God!

All time his own, and all eternity,
With Death, dear Death, an open gate to life,
Where joy fulfills its capability,
And knowledge limitless as joy is rife;
God walks wherever human feet have trod;
There, there is God!

MY HERITAGE

The great of every clime are mine,
  Apostles, prophets, of all time,
  All who have wrought, in prose or rhyme,
To make my life more fit and fine.

Mine too the present, with its joy,
  Its crosses yielding sweetest peace,
  Its daily toil and night's surcease,
Its golden love without alloy.

The coming days I too may claim,
  Nor fear their clouds will rain me ill,
  Well knowing they obey His will
Whose ears are deaf to man's defame.

Life too is mine,—a gracious boon,—
  This breathing, acting, knowing life,
  Its holy calm, its bitter strife,
Defeats, its triumphs late or soon.

And, as the crown of all, fond death,
  Whose kiss at last unveils mine eyes,
  What time glad heaven's sweet surprise
Shall rap away my ravished breath.

PENTECOST

FULFILL, O gracious God, to-day,
  Thy promise made long ages since:
All flesh shall share the Spirit's sway,
  The young, the old, the poor, the prince.

Why delve we in a hoary past,
  For footprints of thy stately tread?
Why hear no more, in all the vast,
  The Voice that wakes the living dead?

The Vision granted but to age,
  Grant thou to youth, of courage strong;
So shall be writ a glory-page,
  In righting every human wrong.

The Spirit's power outpour, we pray,
  Upon all flesh, sin-blind and lost;
Touch every soul with his bright ray,
  Make every day a Pentecost.

A CALIFORNIA DAY

Blossoms of almonds and blossoms of snow!
Almonds a-bloom, yonder, row upon row;
Green on the hillside in billows of grass,
Yielding to snow as still upward you pass;
See what a picture God paints on the screen,
White all the border and green all between!

Where shall you go for a picture like this?
Not to the Eastland of childhood and bliss;
But to the land of the Sunshine, where rain
Whitens the mountains while greening the plain,
Bringing the blossoms to gladden our sight,
White on the almonds and white on the height!

Heart of the lark is a-thrill with a song,
Knowing the rain will not last very long;
Robins are courting, since Spring is at hand,
Time for home-making in all the bird-land!
Sunshine one moment and shadow the next,
Each a glad blessing; ah! who could be vexed?

Bees on a-scurry for nectar, so soon,
Need, sadly need, both a great coat and shoon;
Cheer up, my hearties, for now the sun peeps,
He who has courage a rich harvest reaps.
All kinds of weather a March day can bring;
Easy to sorrow, but better to sing.

ADVERSITY

The mist was heavy on the mountain, where
  I walked alone, and thought of God as near,
Till, huge and threatening, loomed a monster
      there
  Full in my face, and I was filled with fear.

Nearer it came and larger seemed to grow,
  My heart beat faster and I turned to flee,
When a stray zephyr cleared the mist, and lo!
  The monster was a man, like unto me!

I called, he answered merrily, and came
  To where I stood, with God not far away;
Long years had changed him, but he spoke his
      name—
  My brother, lost to me for many a day!

IN MEMORIAM
OF MAJOR J. A. SLADEN

How fares the soldier, now his work is done,
And we have joined in saying: "Well done!
    Well done!"
Sad that no more his presence we may share,
Glad that no more his pain he has to bear?

High converse must he have with some he knew,
And wrought with, when our boys were garbed
    in blue;
With Lincoln, Grant and Sherman, and the rest;
With Howard whom he knew and loved the best.

Brave men and true were they, and found their
    life
In losing it in Freedom's holy strife;
He was a kindred soul to kingly men,
And finds his own as surely now as then.

But far above all men of such degree,
The Captain of Salvation, honored he;
Served Him in serving well his Church and
    State,
And so is with Him in his high estate.

Sore loss we know, yet would not call him back
From such high service, to supply our lack;
But we would pray: Lord, may we worthy be,
Through patient toil, to join his company!

THE SECOND GLORY

Always a second, after the first,
  With a space for gray between,
The sunset comes to a second birth,
  And a greater marvel, I ween;
Deny it who can, since time began
  Has the sun twice said: "Good-by,"
And, craving pardon, I think I can
  Give the proper reason why.

For there's a poppy down in the vale,
  The pride of the Golden State,
And a rose there is by the Lover's Trail,
  And a lily that cried: "Too late!
We were not bright with our tinting, quite,
  The pattern was snatched before!
'Twill take so little to make it right!"
  So, the sunset flames once more.

And there's a ruby high on a cliff,
  That lacks just a dash of red,
And a shell lies on the Morocco Riff;
  With something to add, 'tis said,
But the Master of Art has a kindly heart,
  And He loves perfection so,
That He bids the gray again depart,
  And the glory come, and go.

The man with the hoe did not look up,
    When the West was first a-flush,
And one, alas, was draining the cup,
    And missed the crimson blush,
So the Master of Men brings it back again,
    That no one may fail to see
His marvelous love for His children, when
    He thus says: "Come unto Me."

A CALIFORNIA STORM

THE wind blows from the southland,
  The rain beats on the pane,
The foam flies o'er the gray strand,
  The wreckers reap their gain.
The clouds rift for a second,
As if an angel beckoned,
Or life with death had reckoned,
  And then close up again.

The snow falls on the mountains,
  In fierce and blinding sheets,
It hideth all the fountains,
  And whitens all the steeps;
Lost flocks the shepherd seeketh,
And only sorrow meeteth,
For not a stray lamb bleateth
  Or down the mountain leaps.

The hills take on in gladness
  A livid, vivid green,
That drives away all sadness,
  As to the clouds they lean.
The lowlands long have waited,
But now with joy are mated,
And with the floods are sated,
  That glisten in their sheen.

The valleys laugh in flowers,
  The hills all clap their hands,
The orchards send their showers
  Of perfume o'er the lands;
The bee is drunk with nectar,
The bird, for love, an actor,
And wingèd life the factor
  That shimmers o'er the sands.

Our God the fierce storm sendeth,
  The blinding hail and snow;
The solid earth He rendeth,
  The mountain peaks—they glow.
His ways are past our guessing.
He sendeth sweet refreshing,
And all that is distressing;
  To-morrow we shall know.

OPPORTUNITY

"The same is desert," stark and lone and drear;
No happy voice of children, ringing clear;
No mother busy in the household way,
No sight of human face, the live-long day!

Why should a man forsake the city space,
Where thousands throng, rapt of his word and
    face,
And seek the harvest in the desert lone,
Where no one plows, nor ever seed is sown?

But in the Eunuch, Ethiopia
Is stretching forth her hands to God, to-day;
You leave the thousands in the city mart,
For untold millions, groping in the dark.

The rose of opportunity will bloom
E'en in the desert, for who, late or soon,
Runs thither, thereto led by mandate clear:
"The desert call, away; no 'nay,' no fear!"

THE GLORY OF THE CHRIST

THEIR names unknown, their faces never caught
    By cunning artist and on canvas flung,
That future ages might at least be taught
    How looked the men who this encomium won.

"The glory of the Christ"—such and no less
    The men sent forth on embassy of grace,
To bear to Jewish Christians in distress
    The lavish bounty of an alien race.

'Twas Paul who said it of them, and his pen
    Was guided by a Spirit all divine.
It surely were a joy to know such men,
    And claim them truly as dear friends of mine!

And yet such men are living even now!
    Yea, many, all unknown to name and fame;
No glory nimbus rests upon their brow,
    And dull to many seem their lives, and tame.

But they are loving, as did those of old,
    The Christ who bought them with His dying
       love,
And they are bringing back unto His fold
    Those who shall wear white robes in heaven
       above.

They too are faithful, though small things and
    few
The Master hath committed to their care.
They too are earnest, loving, kind and true
    In making life to others look more fair.

Lord, open Thou mine eyes, that I may see
    In such "The glory of the Christ" to-day!
And help me so to live that I may be
    "The glory of the Christ," as others say.

CONSUMMATION

When the fierce love of life loosens grip,
Pleasures pall, petty cares grow unfit,
As the flush of the sunset flames high
When we wave to the world our good-by,
Then the universe shows a kind face,
And the earth seems to sink to a base,
Whence we leap to the life limitless,
And a share in the Infinite Bliss.

AN ASTEROID

At last, presto, a change,
That ends thy timeless range!
Born eons since, of God, a mist of fire,
And swirled forth to and fro,
Into a sun to grow,
Through fierce affinic force of wild desire,

Which hurtling through vast space
At length didst run its race,
So burst its mighty heart with passion's heat,
And scattered far and wide,
Its million parts aside,
Each seeking fit companion, as was meet;

Thou, sightless speck, didst feel
The pull, for ill or weal,
Of this blind world our tired footsteps tread!
A flash, as if to say:
"A kiss I throw thy way
For I have sought thee long, and now I wed!"

Thus mortals, heart to heart,
Draw near and play their part
One instant in God's great eternity;
Then night resumes its sway
Forever and for aye;
A kiss, then deathless Death for thee and me!

Nay, thou dost still persist,
Ethereal now, a mist
Of fire, as when thou hadst thy primal birth.
So death shall be for me
Added felicity,
A wingèd spirit, freed from fettering earth!

GOD'S WHISPERED NAME

I THINK the sweetest thing in heaven will be
  The New Name, granted when I see His face,
  And with heart-rapture His dear feet em-
      brace—
God's whispered name, known but to Him and
      me!

A secret name throughout eternity,
  That He who only knows me thoroughly
  Shall give because it fits me perfectly,—
God's whispered name known but to Him and
      me!

Sometimes I long to know what it will be,
  Forgetting I may make it what I will,
  If I but hourly His sweet will fulfill—
God's whispered name, known but to Him and
      me!

Long years in earning it I seem to be,
  And thoughtless oft how every wish and deed
  But swells the pile of which that name is
      meed—
God's whispered name, known but to Him and
      me!

GOD'S INHERITANCE IN THE SAINTS

AND can it be that God finds gain in those
   For whom He sent His Son—a ransom, free?
And does He value friends who once were foes?
   And is He rich because possessing me?

Great wealth has He in Nature's amplitude,
   In forests, meadows, landscapes passing fair!
Nay, worlds on worlds, a vast infinitude!
   How can He for a sinner really care?

Oh, vain and foolish! Look within thine heart.
   Thou are not rich in that which has an end.
Dost thou not hold the treasures of the mart,
   As dust and ashes when compared with
      friend?

And is God less than man in this regard?
   Give answer, thou, the heir of every age!
Is He to us exceeding great reward?
   We are to Him a precious heritage!

Up then, O Soul, since God so values thee!
   Dear must thou be to self, since dear to Him.
Walk thou erect, triumphant, brave and free!
   Run swift the race, with strong unfettered
      limb.

REVEALING GOD

No man hath seen our God, says one;
   Revealed alone by Him is He
Whom we may well believe his Son,
   Of Virgin born to set us free.

Forever dwelleth He within
   The bosom of our God above.
He winneth us from every sin,
   Proclaiming ever: God is love!

Before all worlds were made, was He.
   When worlds exist no more, will be.
Revealer, timeless, without cause,
   In Him the face of God we see.

Would you, in any wise, God show,
   To eyes grown blind through dust and din?
Like Christ you too God's heart must know,
   By dwelling evermore within.

In vain you delve in learned tome
   To learn of God, uplifted high.
In vain you beat your flesh and moan
   To find Him out, who yet is nigh.

He dwells within the contrite heart,
   In Him must dwell the heart contrite.
You show Him forth in hall and mart,
   In Christ's own way—by living right.

High art is this, work all sublime,
　　Revealing God to all below!
The one condition—heart of mine,
　　Is living in God's heart, you know.

MY BLESSING

Could I but choose the blessing, fit and fine,
From all those given by Moses ere he died,
I think that Joseph's portion should be mine,
Since with it every other were supplied.
"Of Him who dwelt within the bush, good will!"
What need of mine can not such blessing fill?

What though the flame be fierce, if God be there,
No smallest hair of mine shall shriveled be.
The bush was not consumed on Horeb, where
God spoke with Moses, who drew near to see.
No smell of fire was known when forth they
     came
From that huge furnace there on Shinar's plain.

If I enjoy the good will of that Friend,
Who dwelt within the bush in form of fire,
No threatening clouds whatever they portend
Can rain me aught save what I most desire.
The alchemy of heaven shall change all ill
To blessing, every want of mine to fill.

THE BEST WINE LAST

So Thou wouldst deal with me, O Master, mine!
Let not my lips refuse Thy best of wine!
Nor deem, however rich the blessing now,
Thy grace will not a richer gift allow.

Thrice shame upon me that I ever dream
A cup of mine can drain the flowing stream!
That giving renders less the Giver's power,
Or that withholding can increase His dower.

Oh heart that He hath blest beyond thy meed,
Canst thou not know a higher, deeper need?
Rest not content with blessing that is past,
The Master keeps the best wine for the last.

THE CROSS

For me, didst Thou, my Lord, the heavy cross
  Endure, and utter loss?
For me didst drink such bitter cup of woe,
  That woe I might not know?
The stripes that I deserved didst on Thee fall?
The Father hid his face, when Thou didst call?

No cross have I, since for me Thou hast died,
  For me wast crucified!
Yet in Thy word, such words as these I see:
  "If thou wouldst follow Me,
Take up thy cross! Who seeks his life to save,
The same shall lose! Give thou, even as I
      gave!"

And can there be, dear Lord, Gethsemane,
  And Calvary for me?
Will God, the Father, such a bitter cup,
  Press to my lips to sup?
Oh! strengthen my weak faith, and make me
      know,
Thou walkest with me, all the way of woe!

THE HEARING EAR

Lose not, oh soul of mine, the hearing ear!
When that is lost, is loss excluding hope!
Still God may call, but thou no longer hear,
Nor walk with Christ the long and toilsome
    slope.

Thou will not, when the hearing ear is lost,
Obey the summons, ringing full and free:
"Forth to the vineyard, counting not the cost;
There's work for all, why shouldst thou idle
    be?"

Nor shalt thou hear Him, when at close of day,
He bids thee cease from toil, in welcome rest:
"Come unto me, thou weary one, and lay
Thy heavy, aching head upon my breast!"

When loved ones fade and vanish from thy
    view,
And sorrow sighs in vain: "Would they were
    near!"
Small is thy courage and thy comforts few,
If thou hast lost, oh soul, the hearing ear!

Though fierce temptations ask thee to forget
Thy sorrow in the cup, or lose thyself
In busy marts of trade, and thy regret,
What solace shalt thou find in sordid pelf?

And as the night draws on when no man works,
The shadows thicken fast, thine eye grown dim,
And the gaunt specter at thy doorway lurks,
E'en though He call, how shalt thou come to
　　Him?

Nor shalt thou hear the welcome words: "Well
　　done!
Thou good and faithful servant, enter thou
Into rewarding joy! Thy race is run!"
Nor feel the victor's palm upon thy brow!

Lose not, oh, soul of mine, the hearing ear,
When that is lost, is loss excluding hope!
God calls thee now; fail not, fail not to hear,
And walk with Christ the long and toilsome
　　slope!

WELCOME SONG

WHAT news dost thou bring, sweet one,
  New-born to our earthly ways,
From the land beyond the sun,
  Where the angels stand at gaze,
Ere they start on their mercy run?
  What news, for our humdrum days?

Are the heavens still glad and strong?
  Are our loved ones still content?
Are they chanting still the song,
  That they learned when first they went
From the earthly stress and wrong,
  And left us sore forespent?

Was the melody too grand
  For thy tender ears, sweet child?
And so to a tamer land
  Art thou come, and a mother mild?
Didst thou tire of the Golden Strand,
  And the river undefiled?

Didst thou crave a father's smiles,
  In the land of pure delight,
So was wooed by loving wiles
  To take thy earthward flight
Through the long cathedral aisles
  Of stars, trailing robes of light?

Mid the myriad heavenly host,
  Couldst thou find no mother dear,
Who could make of thee her boast,
  And coo for but thee to hear,
Such songs are known at most
  But to earth, with its love and fear?

Not so good as the heavenly land,
  Yet sweet is the earthly bliss!
Be content from the pearly strand
  To abide for our joy in this!
Weave around our hearts love's band!
  Woo our lives from all amiss!

THE UNKIND KINDNESS

How sharper than a serpent's tooth is bare
Ingratitude! And yet a sharper pang
Shall pierce the heart sore wounded by a friend,
When he, to salve a conscience ill at ease
O'er rank injustice unacknowledged still,
Shall proffer gift, as though such speechless
    thing
Could bring again the frank and open smile,
On lips too white with anguish for a word,
Save such as blisters in the utterance.
Ye Gods, smite with your fiercest flame of wrath,
The age-long insult that a kindness plans
To ichor o'er the wound unkindness wrought,
Yet wants the courage to confess, and crave
A free forgiveness for sweet pity's sake.

A LINK IN THE CHAIN

THE journey may be long through desert sand,
The giants fierce and many you may meet,
Yet shall you enter not the promised land;
You find the Eshcol grapes; you do not eat.

You plant the tree, another plucks the fruit;
You dig for water, others drink the same;
The song you write is sung when you are mute;
You win the fight, another wins the fame.

You too pluck fruit when others sowed the seed;
You plant your feet where others cut the road;
Dim ages spent in toil that you might read!
The iron yoke, the thumb-screw and the goad.

A link you are, no more and no whit less,
In that long chain that reaches from the clod,
Through worm and beast to man; through pain-
    ful guess,
To truth and beauty and the throne of God.

Enough for you to labor, sure of this
That so you help your fellow up the hill.
Of old One said, "This is My food and bliss,
To hear My Father's voice and do His will."

PLUTARCH'S MEN

PLUTARCH painted men heroic,
Warrior, poet, statesman, stoic.
    Such men still you find,
    Have you Plutarch's mind.

Plutarch gave us men of daring;
So are Smith, and Jones, and Waring,
    Be you only wise,
    See you through his eyes.

Plutarch's men loom through the ages,
Grand, majestic; judges, sages;
    They crowd every mart
    Find you Plutarch's heart.

Plutarch's men of light and leading
Still are meeting the world's needing,
    See you sane and whole,
    Have you Plutarch's soul.

"THE OUTSKIRTS OF THY WAYS"

Sharp eyes had they, though veiled with ample
  wing
Before the Holy One—the seraphim
Who in the courts of heaven were heard to sing
In antiphon, surpassing earthly hymn:

"In fullness of the earth Thy glory shows;
Thou art the Holy One, inhabiting,
The heights supernal! From Thy finger flows
All life, and high and low Thy praises sing!"

Ah, yes, Great God! The world indeed reveals
Thy skill and might; Thy wisdom and Thy love!
And yet to mortal eyes, Thy world conceals,
And tempers all that cometh from above.

Dim eyes have we, and blinded by Thy light;
Nor can our ears endure Thy full-toned voice.
How small a whisper hear we of Thy might.
Nor can we see Thee now and yet rejoice!

Hide still Thy glory, lest we fail and sink
Beneath the revelation premature!
We are but children, teach us how to think
How near Thou art, and yet such thought en-
  dure!

Our faltering footsteps lead unto the height
By slow degrees, till we can bear to gaze
On all Thy glory, majesty and might.
Enough to-day "the outskirts of Thy Ways."

THE NORTH STAR

How loyally thou standest at thy post!
The comet flames a month and speeds away
Upon its grand elliptic, sheeted ghost
To fright some other world, some other day.
The meteors flash an instant on the eye
Expiring glory, and then leave the sky.

All other stars but circle in their plane,
Nor hold to human eye an hour their place,
Rising and falling, as moons wax and wane,
Nay, and burn out, when they have run their
     race;
But thou, North Star, alone of all the host,
Art ever true in holding still thy post.

Teach us thy secret, O thou steadfast sun,
And may we emulate thy power and poise.
We fight one day, and on the next we run,
Attain one height, then sink to lower joys.
May Duty be our Pole Star, flaming bright
Upon our path, how dark soe'er the night!

A DAY

A RED, red rose in the East,
That fades to a lily of white,
As the toilers fare forth to their feast,
And God says to the stars, "Good night."

NOON:

A pause in the thick of the strife,
While the toilers take breath, as is meet,
And the Sun, God's chief toiler in life,
Blinds the earth with his billows of heat.

NIGHT:

A passion flower in the West,
That blushes, then pales to a pall,
As the toilers come glad to their rest,
And God whispers, "Good night," to us all.

THE BIRD SONG

As rolls the world around, for aye,
New lands wake ever into day,
From which breaks forth the matin song
Of happy birds who know no wrong.

Perpetual praise thus greets God's ear,
While man sleeps on, too dull to hear;
From East to West it sweeps along,
Recurrent, jubilating song.

The isles of palm first catch the strain,
And gladly waft it o'er the main;
The highest peak receives it now,
And sends it to a lower brow.

Then vales awake in joyful mirth,
That spans the river, lake and firth;
Katahdin echoes on the sound,
Niagara scarce avails to drown.

Vast Western prairies next awake;
And Rocky Mountains seem to quake
Beneath the torrent melody,
That o'er them rolls, majestic, free!

Sierras catch the glad refrain,
Anon, the Sacramento plain;
Pacific Islands clap their hands
And toss the hymn to alien lands.

Thus daily round the earth is flung
    The song that first in Eden rung.
Oh, soul, thy guilty silence break.
    The bird-song bids thine own awake.

GRANDMOTHER'S CONFESSION

So long I wait His coming! Surely He,
Who said, "I will prepare a place for thee,"
Must have, I fear, long since forgotten me!

Or haply He is spending loving care
Beyond His wont to make exceeding fair
The mansion to which I am the sole heir.

I wonder what will be its shape and size?
I hope, and yet I know I am not wise,
Some dear and common things will greet my
    eyes.

I am not used to much that's over fine;
That broken lute I love because 'twas mine
When I was young and life was in its prime.

This tress of hair I cut from Baby's brow,
And I have worn upon my heart till now,
Could I be glad in heaven without it?   How?

Oh, yes, I know 'tis foolish, but 'tis true,
I tell no other, but I tell it you,
I hope I shall not miss that soft, felt shoe.

Such things grow dearer, day by day, I fear.
What's that? A light! And angels drawing
    near!
I think I'm going! good-by, good-by, dear!

GRANDFATHER'S CONFESSION

You ask if I am thinking much of heaven,
  Now I am very old,
And of the many mansions there,
  Within the Shepherd's fold,
And of the crystal walls and gates,
  Of which we have been told;

If I am tired of living here,
  And greatly long to see
The special place my dearest Lord
  In love prepares for me,
And what I think the fruit is like
  That grows upon that tree.

Well, no, my boy, I think far more
  About a fairer past,
When I was young and used to sail
  My boat with tiny mast
And yards and boom, and pebble
  For an anchor to hold fast.

The crystal wall may be right high,
  And bright the pearly gates;
What would I give if I could see
  Once more the pillared mates
That marked the entrance to our barn,
  Festooned with chains and weights!

Twelve kinds of fruit upon one tree
    To me seems very strange;
A tree grew in the pasture, where
    Our sheep were used to range,
Whose fruit I should not care to give
    In any fair exchange.

Oh, yes, I'm old and deaf and blind,
    Nor can I run and leap,
And yet I love my life, as they
    Who never learned to weep;
But hark! I hear the angels call,
    And lay me down to sleep.

FRIENDSHIP

I THINK through all the music of the years,
In which the heart of man has glorified
The name of friend, when he has run his race,
No truer, deeper, nobler note has tolled
Than that by David struck when Jonathan
Upon the Mountains of Gilboa lay,
Slain by the enemies of Israel's God.
How glories he, the youthful warrior bold,
In all the prowess of those men of might—
Saul of the lion-heart and Jonathan,
A worthy son of hardly worthy sire!
"The bow of Jonathan, it turned not back,
The sword of Saul, it did not empty come
From feasting on the blood of mighty men,
From eating up the fat of those they slew!"

It is the wild untutored cry of joy
Upspringing from the savage heart of man,
Untouched by grace of Christian, pitying love,
At sight of foes by Justice stricken down!

"Lovely and pleasant were they in their lives,
And in their death they not divided were!
Swifter were they of foot than eagle's wing!
Stronger were they of arm than lion's paw!
Weep, O ye daughters of our nation, weep!
Weep ye for Saul, who gave your scarlet robes,
And ornaments of gold on you bestowed!"

So soon in face of death, could he forget,
The oft repeated wrong of that great king
Who matched not with great heart his stalwart
    frame,
But once and twice and thrice had fain struck
    dead
Him who had for him nothing now but praise!

"How are the mighty in the battle slain!
And Jonathan, upon the mountains high!
I am distressed for thee, O brother mine!
Thy love, no less than wonderful it was!
Surpassing that of gentle womankind!"
So sweet and pure and simple are the words
In which the youthful David magnifies
The friendship of the man who rightly stood
Between himself and fame as Israel's king!
So deep and true and noble was the love
He bore the son of Saul and Israel's prince!

Thrice blessed Jonathan in such a friend!
Thrice blessed that his friend so soon became
His eulogist, for so immortal fame
For thirty centuries his name has crowned,
That else had perished quickly from the earth,
And left no trace that he had ever been!
Thrice blessed David in his friendship, now,
For Jonathan, since it can never wane,
Nor grow aught else than perfect and complete,
And he himself be glorified thereby!

'Tis hardly possible had life been spared
To Jonathan for three score years and ten,
That he—the heir to greatness, and this lad,
Called by his father, with his shepherd pipe,
To drive away his melancholy moods,
Had still been knit in bonds of amity,
Through all the years of court intrigue and
    strife,
With all the friends of each always at work
To make fierce rivals those who once were
    friends,
No longer emulous of each other's gains.
Nay, had the prince been ever full content
To shine a star of second magnitude,
With David first and foremost everywhere,
Still must these faithful friends of early days,
Have grown apart, as grew the burdens great
That rested on his shoulders they called King,
And cares of state preoccupied his mind,
From which the legal king was all exempt.

For friendship can endure the shock of change,
But when both parties thereto change alike,
And growth keeps pace with growth in lines that
    move
Forever onward, side by side, secure.
We grow apart from friends of early days
Because we grow diversely, one this way,
One that, with diverse tastes and aptitudes
That differ widely with the widening years.

The saddest meeting this side gates of doom,
Is when two friends, in open hearted youth,
Long sundered by the years that change us so,
Once more are thrown into each other's arms,
To find, alas, no heart-doors open now,
Nor aught in common whence new confidence
May germinate to soothe the ache of years.
We pledge eternal fealty in our dawn,
Resolve and re-resolve that nothing now
Shall ever come between our hearts and those
To whom we open all our richest store!
But Fate stands by, a curl upon her lip!
Blind eyes has she, and yet she clearly sees
The havoc time and space and differing aims
Will wreak upon our pledged fidelity!

"Great souls by instinct to each other turn,
Demand alliance and in friendship burn?"
Yes, this is true as it is finely told!
But though thy soul be great as that of Paul,
And some great Barnabas thou callest friend,
Yet shalt thou see him choose another self,
And set his sail upon some sunset sea,
While you with other friend shall journey forth,
Never again to solder sundered bonds,
Unless you grow incorporate, each in each,
Not separate and diversely, one from one.
To keep a friendship strong from dawn to
      prime,
From prime to sunset of the earthly span,

Each party thereto must keep step with each,
In growth of mind and heart and will and soul.

And yet the whole of truth on this high theme
Is not thus fully, adequately told.
The truest friendship some have ever known
Has been with horse or cat or faithful dog,
By Nature fated to a changeless round.
The highest friendship man can ever form
Is with that Being throned above the stars,
Who groweth not to other with the years.
Seek deep enough within the scale of life,
Soar high enough on wings of faith and trust,
You shall discover one at each extreme
That changing not permits a change in you,
Nor shall linked bonds dissolve in deep regret.

Your poor dumb friend to which you yield your
        heart,
Because perchance none other seeks the prize,
And you must have one confidant or die,
Proves faithful to you from the first to last,
Because he cannot change from less to more,
Nor does he see that you are not the same
To-day as when he yielded you his heart.
If he could know you change from less to more,
You two fast friends would soon be sundered
        far,
And such a compact prove as short a truce
As any ever struck with human kind.

One says—"If 'twere not for my cat and dog,
I think I could not live another day."
One says it, but its echo strikes a chord
In hearts responsive over all the earth,
Since this Rialto where we barter hearts
Is crossed by multitudes companionless,
Save in the order lower than mankind.

And in this mart the rich are not more blessed
Than are the poor, since what the cynic prates:
"The rich have many friends, the poor but few,"
Is false as are all fancies Satan-born.
Say not to some who roll in lavish wealth:
"There are no dogs in heaven," if you would
     fain
Persuade them seek an entrance thereto.
'Tis not alone the Indian who hopes
That "once admitted to that equal sky,
His faithful dog shall bear him company."
Nor yet alone those who are poor in purse,
Who never open heart to kindred heart,
But find in cat or dog or horse sole friend.
The lower order yieldeth friends that last,
Since rooted firm in hopeless ignorance.

There is a Friend that sticketh closer than
A brother, who is oft no friend at all!
In youth and prime and age He faithful is.
He knoweth all, so cannot wiser grow;
He willeth all, so cannot grow more firm;

He filleth all, so cannot come to more.
He too to-morrow will be just the same
As yesterday, as will your poor dumb pet.
All yesterdays with Him are known as Now;
As Now are all to-morrows open laid.
He changeth not as Friend, since change there
    is
With Him in nothing; rooted firm is He
In perfect wisdom, perfect truth and grace.

"If all the gentlest hearted friends I know"—
So writes the woman Robert Browning loved:
"Concentered in one heart their gentleness,
That still grew gentler till its pulse was less
For life that pity, I should yet be slow
To bring my own heart nakedly below
The palm of such a friend, that he should press
Motive, condition, means, appliances,
My false ideal joy and fickle woe,
Out full to light and knowledge; I should fear
Some plait between the brows, some rougher
    chime
In the free voice: O angels, let your flood
Of bitter scorn dash on me! do ye hear
What I say, who bear calmly all the time
This everlasting face to face with God?"
Why bear the angels calmly all the time
An everlasting face to face with God?
Because they're perfect, never having sinned?
Nay, this is not the reason, since frail man,

[79]

A sinner from his youth, redeemed by grace,
Can bear to look upon his God, nor blanch.
It is because they know He knows it all,
It is because we know He knows it all,
That they and we are not afraid to tell
The God of all the uttermost of self,
Which we would fain keep back from other
     friend.

An ideal friend were one to whom we dare
Throw open wide the innermost recess
Of all we are, have been and hope to be.
Hence God alone to man is ideal Friend.
For surely only Him dare we tell all;
He and our poor dumb friend, that hears our
     words,
But understands them not, nor can repeat.
God pity those whose one sole friend on earth
Is found within the brute creation's ranks,
Forever true, since, fated to remain
Forever stagnant, knowing naught of growth!
God pity those who find no Friend in Him
Who cannot grow away from those He loves,
Since He too groweth not from less to more,
But was and is and evermore shall be
Complete and whole, so progress need not make!

Shall we who value friendship more than gold,
Since it hath yielded us more rich content,
Shall we put down as so much treasure lost

All those who started equals in life's race,
Who now pass by us with averted face?
Nay, surely, some friends lost are richest gain.
If one has grown less noble with the years,
Less open to the vision heaven grants
In those rare moments, when we pierce her
    depths,
It were a crime to call him still the friend
He was when climbing with you heights of
    power,
And delving with you into learning's store.
You may be friendly to him now as then,
And yet no friend companioning his aims.
Nor should you breathe regret, save for his sake,
That he has fallen behind you in the race.

Perchance you pass some friend of better days
With face averted, conscious you have failed
In reaching heights he is at home upon.
Why should you breathe regret, his friendship
    lost,
Save for yourself, no longer worthy it?
To keep a friendship with a worthy man,
You must keep up with him in worthy ways,
Nor lag behind him when he beckons on
To fields untrodden by reluctant feet.
Nor should you seek a friendship, save with
    those
Who spur you on to something not attained
By those that drift upon the tides of life.

[81]

Seek ever those who climb from less to more,
And count your wealth by such, who call you
    friend.
Success in life is measured by friends lost;
Success in life is measured by friends won;
Since each new plane touched by your feet and
    kept
Shall prove some loss, may prove a richer gain.
It were a shame in you, if well content
To be to-morrow what you are to-day,
It were a shame to clog the climbing feet
Of one you call a friend, if he has heard
The voice that ever shouts "Excelsior!"
Nay, let him on, while you heart-compact form
With one content to take no further step
In growth of mind and heart and will and soul.

It is a saying old and quaint and true:
"In building friendship we can not suppose
So brave a pile should out of nothing grow."
If you are poor in friends, though rich in pelf,
It is because there nothing in you is
To which true friendship may attach itself.
Your poverty in friends is solely due
To poverty in heart and character.
Chide not blind Fate that all have friends but
    you;
Chide your own self unworthy such a boon.

"In friendship see we only faults which may
Be prejudicial to the one named friend.

In love we see no faults but those by which
We are ourselves made conscious of some loss."
If this be true, as many do insist,
Then friendship true is seen a richer boon
Than human love was, is, or e'er can be.
It needs must have some modicum of truth
Or it would find no voice in many tongues.
This sure is true, the things that pain us most
In those most worthy naming as our friends,
Are things that injure them, and not ourselves;
Some fleck or flaw that makes them suffer loss
In other's eyes or in the eyes of God;
Some taint, that clinging to them through all
      time,
Shall make them less through all eternity.

And surely this is true, that some deny
The things in us that pain our gracious God,
Are those that mar us, warp as from life's aims.
A yelping dog cannot insult a man,
Nor injure his renown and dignity.
A sinning man cannot insult his God,
Nor injure Him, as man can injure man.
Our sin grieves Him because it injures us.
He stands not on his honor, as do some
Who jealous are of their supposèd rights.
Sin 'gainst our God is sin against ourselves,
And so is hateful to Him, since our Friend.
For read we not aright the scroll of grace:
"Consider Him who patiently endures

Such contradiction of sinners against them-
    selves"!
So great the pain God knows when we do that
Which mars us, warps us from life's nobler aims.

The greatest honor yet shown man by God
Was shown to that great Hebrew, Abraham,
When, a millennium after he had died,
God speaking by a greater prophet, said,
Of him of mighty faith: "HE is my friend."
The greatest honor, save when God's own Son,
In whom the Father stands revealed in full,
Said to the Twelve whom He had servants
    called:
"Henceforth I call you friends, not servants
    more,
For all things have I now revealed to you,
Revealed to me by Him whose will I do."

And yet such honor may be shared by all
Who will to do and so to learn His will.
For still the Son reveals to such the things
Of God, whereby they grow to be God-like,
God's secrets, shared alone by friends of God,
Whom He is not ashamed to call "My friends."

And is it not a glad and blessed thought,
These days when friendship meaneth much to
    all,
That howsoever few the friends we know

On earth, or in the heavens, where they wait,
And watch our coming with expectant eyes,
God is our Friend, though we may be his foe?
He sees with larger, other eyes than ours.
Though man find nothing of prime worth in us,
To which he may reveal his inner self,
So calling us his friend, yet He, our God,
Who formed us in His image, for Himself,
Finds something in us worthy His regard.
He is our Friend, and fain would prove to us
His friendship, leading us to call Him ours.

How may this Friend, unseen forevermore,
'Till like Him, we shall see Him as He is—
How shall He prove to us his friendship here?
Nay, that He is at all, and not a dream?
We are so blind to what our eyes see not,
So occupied and overwrought with care,
So full of this and that in search of joy,
We have no time for friendship with our God.

But He has time, and soon or late a Hand,
Is laid upon us, which we needs must feel.
Then this and that which long have seemed so
      large
Grow suddenly to be of little worth;
And how, since blind, to find our unseen Friend
Becomes a question fraught with tragic fate!

Long search have some for Him who dwells
    afar,
And yet who walketh ever by our side,
And worketh in our mind and heart and will;
And oft they cry: "O that I understood
How Him to find, that I might even come
Unto His seat! Why standeth God afar?"

God dwells indeed in the far distant heavens,
And with the humble and the contrite heart,
And unto thee and me and him we meet,
He ever says: "Me shall ye seek and find
When ye shall search for Me with all your
    heart."
And when we find Him, He doth bring us
    straight
Unto his house of banqueting, and spreads
Above us there the banner of his love.

So great the love of Saul's son for his friend,
As his great heart was fitted to possess;
So great the love his eulogist bore him,
As towered his nature over that of Saul.
The heart of God is infinitely great;
And there's a chamber there no one can fill
Save you alone; so enter and find rest.

THE ROCK THAT FOLLOWED

FIRM as the everlasting rock, we say
Whene'er we wish to picture forth in words
Stability unmoved of stress or shock.
Nor wants there poet who hath finely said:
"How massively doth awful nature pile
The living rock, like some cathedral aisle
Sacred to silence and the solemn sea."
And Job the patient man of Uz exclaims:
"O that my words with iron pen were writ
Upon a rock, secure forevermore."
And yet that Saul whom now we know as Paul,
When speaking of the journeyings forty years,
Of Hebrew freedmen, late Egyptian slaves,
And how on angels' food they long were fed,
Assures us that the Rock did follow them!
A spiritual Rock from which they quenched their
        thirst,
And he makes bold to call this Rock our Christ!

This sure was not the rock that Moses smote
In Horeb with the rod wherewith he cowed
The lordly Nile whose waters blushed to blood,
The rock whence waters gushed forth lavishly
To quench the thirst of all in Rephidim;
For read we not: "And as they journeyed on
They came to Moreh's bitter waters where
The Lord to Moses showed a healing tree,
Which, casting in, the waters were made sweet;

And as they journeyed onward yet again
They came to Elim where were many springs,
And fruitful palm trees glad to drink thereof,
And there encamped and gladly did they drink.
And as they journeyed on they came to Beer,
Which meaneth well, and there so glad were
    they,
They sang this song: "Spring up, spring up,
    O Well,
Well, which the princes digged, and nobles of
The people delved, with scepters and with
    staves."
Songs simple as the childhood of the race,
And sparkling with the freshness of the dawn.
Nay, sure the rock that Moses smote at first,
Remaineth where it stood so long ago,
And Arab fingers itching for your gold,
Still point it out to thirsty pilgrim bands,
That evermore retrace the wanderings
Of those who moved but as the pillar moved,
And rested as it rested on their camp.
And so this Rock that followed where they went,
Those Hebrew freedmen, whom we think so
    gross
And all devoid of finer instincts, tastes,
And apprehension high and spiritual,
Was that same Rock whence we may quench our
    thirst,
If we, like them, have had a taste of God,

And know the joy of those who walked with
    Him,
Nor strive to satisfy our deeper needs
With that which crave but carnal appetites.
"They drank," says Paul, "of Rock that fol-
    lowed them,
A Spiritual Rock, and too that Rock was
    Christ."

And so our Christ was known to men of old,
Long ages ere was born in Bethlehem
The Child whose advent angel voices sang,
With "Peace on earth, and to all men good will";
Was known to men of stubborn hearts and wills,
Who did not fully please our gracious Lord,
And so were not permitted to set foot
Upon that land with milk and honey blessed,
That beckoned to them ever as they went,
While one by one they, weary, laid them down
For their last sleep, within the wilderness.
And so we learn anew the lesson old,
And oft forgotten by our fevered age,
The lesson sweet to be remembered still,
That God hath always spoken through the
    Word,
The Word that once was clothed in human flesh
And walked with men, Himself the Son of Man,
Albeit still the very Son of God.
And does not he, the seer of Patmos, say:
Christ is the Lamb that hath been ever slain

Since the foundation of the world? Again
Doth he not tell us that this Christ he knew
Has, always been the Light enlightening all
Who dwell within creation's utmost bounds?

Full weary certain was the way they trod—
Those Hebrew freedmen, late Egyptian slaves,
And hot the desert sands were to their feet,
And oft they longed to bend their backs again
Beneath the lashes cruel of those who drave
Them to their work of making needed brick
Without the needed straw, since there was food,
Fish they did eat and cucumbers,
And melons, leeks and onions, without stint.
But far within the howling wilderness:
"Our soul," they said, "is dried away, we have
Naught save this manna now to look unto,
And we do loathe this light food, angels love."
And yet to them our gracious God was good,
Remembering their frame, that they were dust,
And as the things of time and sense did wane,
And He did wean them from the lower good,
He ever stirred within them longings deep
For higher things than Egypt's plains can yield,
And thirst they knew that He alone can quench.
They drank from that great Rock that followed
    on,
The Spiritual Rock, whom now we know as
    Christ.
Nay, gracious was our God and merciful

To take away the food they loved the most
That they might eat of spiritual food,
And drink of Christ, the Spiritual Rock.
Far better had it been for those who fell,
Within the waste of howling wilderness,
Had they remained in Pharaoh's fruitful land
To build his treasure cities—Raamses,
And Pithom, than to toil through desert sands
Still on, and on for many years, and die,
The promised land a promise and no more?
Is this the way you read the ancient tale?
And did it count for naught to those who fell
That God did make Himself for forty years
A fiery pillar lighting them by night,
A cloud of glory guiding them by day?
That He did speak to Moses face to face,
As man to-day speaks to his fellow man?
Was it for naught that He did give them food
Convenient for them, duly, morn by morn?
And that our Christ, the Rock, did follow them,
From which they quenched the Spirit's finer
        thirst?
Nay, nay, this surely was a greater good
Than Egypt's gardens, watered by the foot,
Have yielded any race, or then or now.

And so perhaps the promised land for them,
Who never set their foot within its bounds,
Did all that promised land may ever do,
And more for them than for their happier sons,

For whom the promise bore fruition sweet.
Is it not written: "As an eagle bold
Stirs up her nest and flutters o'er her young,
He spread abroad his wings, and on
His pinions bore them. He, the Lord, alone
Did lead them on, nor was a stranger God
Once found among them, all the weary way"?
Is it not written: "The Eternal God
Has ever been thy dwelling place secure,
And underneath, the everlasting arms"?
Is it not written even of those who fell
Within the waste and howling wilderness:
"Who then is like to thee, O Israel,
A people savèd by the Lord, alone,
The shield of all thy help, the sword
Of all thy excellency, thy sole God"?
Not wholly pleasing were the faithless men,
Afraid to enter in where giants were,
Not wholly pleasing, as they bravely tried
When God had said: "I will not go before";
And so they turned and wandered, on and on
For many years within the wilderness;
But not alone they wandered on and on,
Nor all for naught their discipline severe.
God casts not off His people whom He loves,
Nor though they oft forsake, does He forget;
Afflicts them for their profit, be we sure;
And yet so tender-hearted is our God,
He is afflicted as He still afflicts,
And comforted when He can comfort yield.

Like as a father pitieth his sons,
So pities God his children evermore,
Remembering their frame, that they are dust.

And fiery serpents did He send, that bit
His people when they murmured by the way,
In compassing the land by Edom owned?
But did He not, the lesson duly learned,
Command a brazen serpent to be made,
And lifted up in sight of all the host,
That whoso looked, when bitten, still might live?
And when the king of Moab, sore distressed,
Sent for the heathen seer to curse his foes:
"Come curse me Jacob, Israel defy,"
Did not the heathen prophet bless them all?
"How shall I curse whom God hath never
    cursed?
And how defy whom God hath not defied?
Behold I have received command to bless,
For He hath blessed, nor can I hinder it.
Nay, let me die as dies the righteous man,
And my last end, be likened unto His!"
Well does the Hebrew prophet say of old:
"Forgiving Thou didst evermore forgive,
Yet taking vengeance on their doings vile."
The Spiritual Rock that followed ever on
Was Christ our Lord, and all did drink thereof.
Their bones have whitened into dust long since,
Yet they unseen have ever walked with God,

Made fit and meet by walking forty years
With Christ, our Lord, whom now they see and
know.

Their history is parable writ large,
For other ages, other races, climes;
Writ large that he who runs may read and
know.
We too are journeying to a promised land,
Whose margin fades forever as we move;
And we have had our Egypt servitude,
Now broken, yet entreating to return.
For oft the pleasure of the sense defeats
The pleasure of the spirit's walk with God.
And there are desert sands of painful toil,
For all who follow on where duty leads,
And Hope springs up but to be beaten down
In blinding rain of disappointment's tears,
And often Elim's springs and fruitful palms
Prove a mirage but pictured on the sky;
We follow fast but never overtake.
And there are giant sons of Anak too,
That we must fight ere we may win our way
Into the land of promise, just beyond.
Their names are legion, Ignorance and Sloth,
And Lust and Doubt and Fear and Cowardice,
And nameless other dark-browed sons of Night
Dispute our passage onward, inch by inch.
And serpents hiss and bite us unaware,
And friends prove foes, betraying with a kiss.

The good we seek to do oft proves an ill
That better far had still been left undone.
The wicked prosper and the just decline,
And righteousness is fed with penury.
We climb our Pisgahs, where a view is given
Of that fair land beyond the swelling flood,
Then die, as Moses died nor enter in.
Were it not better far had we remained
In Egypt's servitude to blinding sin,
Where there was food sufficient to our need,
Nor longing strange disturbed our calm con-
    tent?

If I speak thus, behold I shall offend
Against the generation of thy children, Lord.
Too painful was it when I thought to know,
Until I went into the house of God.
Then understood I how our gracious Lord
Too wise to err, too kind to be unjust,
Must ever wean us from the lower good
By breaking baubles that our childhood please;
Must ever lead us on with promise fair,
That broken is to earthly sense and sound,
And so its inner spirit made secure;
Must disappoint us oft upon the way,
With fruit that turns to ashes as we eat;
Must teach us as experience only can,
That sin which seems as honey in the mouth,
Soon turns to gall and bitterest regret;
Must chasten us, not for his pleasure, sure,

But for our profit, which if we endure,
Yields as the far-off interest of tears,
The fruits of righteousnss, and peace and joy.
And why do serpents sinful bite us oft,
But that to Him who hath been lifted up,
We may lift up our eyes in faith and live?
Why do we toil through deep and thirsty sands,
Our souls dried up with thirst that's still un-
    quenched,
But that we too from that same Spiritual Rock,
That follows us forever as we move,
May drink as drank God's people, pillar-led?
Why prove but a mirage our Elim's palms
But that we still may travel on and on,
To the ideal, and never overtake?
For surely higher truth still beckons on,
To him who knows the truth that makes him
    free;
And loftier peak lies hidden over there,
With its bold challenge tempting feet that
    climb;
And all the good of earthly sense and sound,
That bids us linger on the heavenward way,
Seems but as dust and ashes when we taste
That which our God reserves for us in store.

Ah, happier far the man who says, "My soul's
Athirst for God, the living God," then he
Who hugs himself in simple sense-content:
"Soul, thou hast goods laid up for many years,

[96]

Eat thou, and drink, and be thou merry too."
Ah, happier he by promises led on
That meet with no fruition, earthly-wise,
If so his feet but tread the narrow way,
Than he who rests at ease by lotus trees
Whose fruit but pleases, while it blasts and
    kills.

The cup the Father giveth us to drink,
Shall we not drink it, as did He, the Son?
And his baptism, shall it not be ours,
If so He wills, who never makes mistake?
And can He not still turn to blessings pure,
The curses those who hate us would pronounce?
And be to us a glory-cloud by day,
And fiery pillar lighting all our night?
We too may sing: "Spring up, spring up, O
    Well,"
Of every pleasure shared with Christ, our King.
Nor shall we miss, if we will have it so,
The Everlasting Arms that comfort yield.
And why meet we the giant Anak's sons,
That tempt our feet into all devious ways,
"But that we may do battle and have praise"?
Ah, yes, you too, long since had entered in

But for your faithless fear of giants strong,
And so were turned to wander on and on
Within the wilderness of pain and doubt;
But not alone you wander on and on,

Since He who led them, leads you ever, too,
And He, the Rock, still follows on the way,
For it is written: "And the Lord thy God
Shall go before thee, and Jehovah, blest,
Shall be thy rear-ward, guarding from all
    harm."

Strange alchemy of heaven surely this,
That our mistakes and failures, yea, our sins,
Transmuted are in crucibles of pain,
To golden crowns that rest upon our heads,
Which eyes anointed see, and so are glad.
Why should we spend our days in vain regret
That we have failed, where others have achieved,
When so a higher good we may achieve,
If we but follow, as He leads us on?
Why should we kick against the goads of God,
That prick us but as we lie down supine,
Or when we wander from the narrow way?
Why should we murmur at the food He gives
Us daily, morn by morning manna sweet,
And thus provoke Him richer food to grant,
Whereof to eat our surfeit and so die?

Nay, let us welcome all that ministers
Unto the spirit's deeper needs and joys,
Nor fail to thank Him when He takes away
That which but hinders, while it seems to help,
And blinds our eyes unto all higher good.
Man surely cannot live by bread alone,

And every word proceeding from our God
Is meat indeed to those who do his will.
The Rock that follows us is Christ, our Lord,
And He has said that whoso asks of Him
Shall living waters drink, and thirst no more.

Ho, every one that thirsteth, come ye, come,
Come to the waters, flowing full and free!
And ye that have no money, come ye, come,
Buy wine and milk, more precious far than gold,
And so are given to all who feel their need!
Why should those Hebrew freedmen, lately
    slaves,
Have tasted waters that our Christ can give,
While you who boast your higher privilege
Still drink at muddy springs that do defile?
Why be a slave and driven by the lash,
Imperious of passions, ever fed,
And clamoring for more as they are fed,
When at so great a price your sovereign Lord,
Has purchased freedom for you and release?
Sure, there is rarer joy in climbing heights
Than you have found in wallowing in mire,
And deeper satisfaction, ministering,
Than those enjoy who still are served by sin.
For he that overcometh eats to-day
The hidden manna and is given power
To rule the nations, and is clothed in white,
Meet symbol of the purity within;
He too is made a pillar in God's house,

And bears the name of God where all can see,
And sits with God upon a throne of power.

Come, says the Spirit, and the Bride says, come,
The church of God, the Wife of Christ, the
    Lamb,
Slain in God's purpose since the world was made,
And known to Hebrew freedom as the Rock
That followed on, from which they quenched
    their thirst;
Come, come, for all things are now ready, come,
The fatlings killed and all the banquet spread.
Why will ye perish in the far-off land,
When in your Father's house is food enough,
And welcome from a heart that mourns your
    loss?

Come, come, let him that hears repeat the word,
To each and all he meets upon the street,
Or in the school or in the marts of trade,
Till nevermore shall there be found a man,
A woman, or a child of tender years,
Who says: "No one there is who cares for me,
Or whether I am saved or still am lost."
Oh, shame upon us, loss beyond compare,
If having tasted that the Lord is good,
We take our rest, nor go into the streets
And highways of the city, saying "Come!"
Oh, shame if having quenched our thirst for
    God,

We seek not everywhere for thirsty souls,
And urge the invitation: "Come, oh, Come!"
Oh, shame if having made our peace with God,
We yet forget souls cursed by inner strife,
Nor win a peace by multiplying peace.

He that hath ears to hear, still let him hear,
And understand, and inwardly digest.

THE JOY OF THE LORD

"THE joy of the Lord"—the joy of toil
Forth reaching to some great and worthy end,
Of aim accomplished, spite of Satan's foil.
Of bane turned blessing and of foe made friend.

The joy of mighty potencies displayed
What time Creation's natal song was sung,
And all the Sons of God, in light arrayed,
Together shouted, till heaven's arches rung.

The joy of seeing ignorance give place
To knowledge, ripening into wisdom sure,
The upward striving of a tethered race
From brutal instincts to humane and pure.

The joy of patient waiting the return
Of those enamored of the ways of sin,
Well knowing they, or soon or late, will learn,
And at the Wicket Gate pray: "Let us in!"

I share such joy? O boon beyond compare!
And faithfulness its sole, sufficient ground?
That I may taste a joy so rich, so rare,
Whate'er my task, I will be faithful found.

AN INTERPRETATION

No God have we when Water, Wind and Fire
Combine to work their havoc and our woe.
In vain our prayers to soften the fierce ire
Of cruel Fate, who stalks forth, to and fro,
Destruction flinging broadcast, everywhere,
And terror hurtling through the frightened air.

Cry louder, frantic worshiper, for see,
Your God is fast asleep, and so will wake,
Or peradventure on a journey, he,
And so his homeward wandering will take.
Alas, it boots not, Famine now we see
Add its bequest to the first fatal Three!

No reckless God have we who breaks his law
That bids the water hasten to the sea,
And forests harbor in their spacious maw
The water's wasteful strength for need to be.
Perhaps the value of a tree we know
Through such swift ruin and dire overflow.

GOD'S JOY

God's joy is sure a joy beyond compare,
A satisfaction waxing more and more!
A universe dependent on his care,
Yet unperturbèd as He was before!
He worketh all things by resistless will,
But effortless is He, and calm and still!

Vast fire-balls, born of fire-mist, forth He hurls
Upon their age-long race through space pro-
    found,
As easy as a maid her ringlet curls
Around her finger! and long eons round,
While patient He awaits their fires' decay,
That He may speak them full of life, some day.

An added joy is born to God what time
A world first yields itself to life new-born,
For now with patience infinite, sublime,
From low to high He sees the spiral form,
Till one appears who stands erect and sings:
"My soul would fly to Thee! Give Thou the
    wings!"

With joy He watches thus a growing race,
Slow struggling upward through mistake and
    sin,
Withholding now, and granting now his grace,
Lest too much help corrupt the life within,

Nor fearful that a foe defeat the plan
Decreed when first He said: "Let there be
    man!"

The joy of incompleteness rounding out
To full completeness—such I ween is Thine,
Thou Father-God! Nor let me ever doubt
That Thou wilt make the pile complete and
    fine;
Though vast eternities may come and go,
They reap the harvest Thou alone didst sow.

Why should I struggle like a prisoned bird
To soar beyond my destined bound and reach?
Or why aspire to speak some lofty word,
When Thou hast granted me but infant speech?
Enough for me to share Thine own rich joy,
In straining out a bit of life's alloy!

THE LESSER LIGHT

No cloud in all the sky, to-night,
No mist nor fog to hide the light,
And yet save one no orb is bright.

A myriad stars last night I saw,
I see no more, they now withdraw
Obedient to another law.

The moon now lords it in the sky,
A tiny ball flung out on high
With borrowed light!   Yet she is nigh.

A rush light she, obscuring quite
All flaming stars!   Since distant light
Is vanquished by the merest mite

Held near the eye, that cannot see
The sun itself though it may be
The fount of light and life to me.

Our Christ is He who everywhere
Enlightens men, on earth, in air,
Or underneath the world, so fair;

And yet his light is oft obscured
By lesser lights, age-long endured,
In custom hardened and inured.

His earthly mother on whose breast
His infant head was laid to rest
What time He started on his quest

The race to save from sin's estate,
And lead back, pure, inviolate,
So fit to enter heaven's gate;

She—Mary—innocent and mild,
And pure and good and undefiled,
So fit for bearing such a child,

Alas, she should for millions be
A light obscuring utterly
The Light who hung upon the tree!

Of one long, long ago Christ said:
I've chosen him, his footsteps led,
Endowed him both in heart and head,

That to the Gentiles he may bear
My Name, so shall they also share
My saving grace, vouchsafed to prayer.

Yet he to many is, I ween,
A light that cometh in between
The soul and Light, a shadowy screen.

Nay, all who undertake to show
The Light of life to all below
Somehow obscure the radiant glow!

Forgive us, majesty divine,
That we, rejoicing to be thine,
And draw thy portrait, line on line,

That other souls may share thy grace,
And bow the head in every place
To Thee—the light of all the race,

Forgive us that the taper small,
We hold to show thy face to all,
Should yet conceal it, like a pall!

Forgive us, that we stand between;
A screen to hide thy light serene,
That to be loved needs but be seen!

PASTURES NEW

When the fierce love of life loosens grip,
Pleasure palls, narrow cares grow unfit,
As the flush of the sunset flames high
When we wave to the world our good-by,
Then the universe shows a kind face,
And the earth shrinks away to the base,
Whence we leap to a life limitless,
And a share in the Infinite Bliss.

SONGS OF THE NIGHT

THEY come to me—Songs of the Night—
From out the silence, deep and blue;
I listen, wishing I might write
Their messages to you, and you!

Songs that the angels sing, for such
As need them most upon the earth;
I listen, if I may but clutch
Within my heart their wonder-worth!

When once again glad day is born,
The angels shimmer into light.
I sit with pen in hand, forlorn;
Their beauty vanishèd with night.

Sometimes the songs of night are set
To melody made by the spheres;
I listen awe-struck, knowing, yet,
It was intended for God's ears!

Sometimes I hear, with not more right,
The song they heard—those faithful men
Who watched their sleeping flocks by night,
Upon the plains of Bethlehem.

It boots not, music such as this
Lives not in garish light of day;
And yet for all, I would not miss
Such holy nights, say what you may!

THE ADDED BURDEN

As I was rushing through the crowded street,
Too eager in my task a soul to greet,
I chanced to see a stranger, stooped and bent
Beneath a heavy burden, and sore spent.
I stayed my footsteps, just a hand to lend,
And, lo, the stranger was my dearest friend!
Long years had passed since I had seen his face.
Now I forgot my eager rushing pace,
And trivial, nay, foolish seemed my quest,
For to his home I went, and tarried as his guest.

Strange thing I find—another's load to bear
Makes mine own lighter, banishes my care!
And so it pleasures me to lend a hand,
Nor idly gaze from some more lofty stand
Upon a fellow mortal's overtask,
While I in snug content and sunshine bask;
And oft a friend I win upon the way
By simply being friendly all the day.
I reach not Jericho as soon as some,
But neither priest nor Levite heard the word:
    "Well done!"

How many anxious faces do we meet
As on we press through all the weary street!
How many harried men and women find
Too full of care to others to be kind!

Oh, weary ways of world and men, we cry,
Is it so needful thus to hurry by?
Will time run out, eternity begin,
If every petty stake you do not win?
Would you but greet and help some other soul,
You might find rest and win at length a nobler
    goal!

CPSIA information can be obtained
at www.ICGtesting.com
Printed in the USA
BVHW040912211218
536170BV00015B/378/P

9 781331 498629